Patricia Nixon

Jill C. Wheeler

ABDO
Publishing Company

visit us at
www.abdopublishing.com

Published by ABDO Publishing Company, 8000 West 78th Street, Edina, Minnesota 55439.
Copyright © 2010 by Abdo Consulting Group, Inc. International copyrights reserved in all
countries. No part of this book may be reproduced in any form without written permission from the
publisher. The Checkerboard Library™ is a trademark and logo of ABDO Publishing Company.

Printed in the United States.

 Manufactured with paper containing at least 10% post-consumer waste

Cover Photo: Library of Congress
Interior Photos: Alamy p. 6; AP Images pp. 12, 17, 20, 27; Corbis pp. 5, 23, 25; Getty Images p. 15;
    Picture History pp. 9, 18, 19; Courtesy of the Richard Nixon Library & Birthplace Foundation
    pp. 7, 10, 11, 13

Series Coordinator: BreAnn Rumsch
Editors: Megan M. Gunderson, BreAnn Rumsch
Art Direction & Cover Design: Neil Klinepier

Library of Congress Cataloging-in-Publication Data

Wheeler, Jill C., 1964-
  Patricia Nixon / Jill C. Wheeler.
      p. cm. -- (First ladies)
  Includes index.
  ISBN 978-1-60453-632-4
 1. Nixon, Pat, 1912-1993--Juvenile literature. 2. President's spouses--United States--Biography--
Juvenile literature. 3. Nixon, Richard M. (Richard Milhous), 1913-1994--Juvenile literature. I.
Title.
  E857.N58W47 2009
  973.924092--dc22
  [B]
                                    2009011251

Contents

Patricia Nixon

Patricia Nixon was First Lady from 1969 to 1974. Her husband was Richard Nixon, the thirty-seventh president of the United States. In 1972, President Nixon became involved in a **scandal** known as Watergate. Two years later, he resigned from office and the Nixons left the White House. This had never happened to a president and First Lady before.

As First Lady, Mrs. Nixon believed in helping others. She supported volunteer work. She also traveled to many countries and offered help to those in need.

Mrs. Nixon was First Lady at a time of great change. During the late 1960s and early 1970s, women spoke up about equal rights. Mrs. Nixon supported their efforts. Yet, she also valued her role as a traditional homemaker.

Mrs. Nixon never wanted to be a political wife. Still, she felt it was her duty to support her husband's career. Mrs. Nixon did not try to influence American policy. As a result, she escaped much of the anger her husband faced after Watergate. Instead, Mrs. Nixon gained respect as a supportive wife and mother.

Patricia Nixon just wanted to be remembered as the president's wife. Yet, she became well known for her work as First Lady.

Farm Life

Over the years, many of Nevada's mining towns have died out. But today, Ely is the largest city in eastern Nevada.

Thelma Catherine Ryan was born on March 16, 1912, in Ely, Nevada. Her father, William "Bill" Ryan, was a miner there. Bill was Irish. He nicknamed his daughter Pat because she was born the day before Saint Patrick's Day. After her father died, she made Patricia her legal name in memory of him.

Pat's mother was Katarina Halberstadt Bender Ryan. She went by Kate. Kate was originally from Germany. She had been previously married. So, Pat had a stepsister and a stepbrother. She also had two older brothers named Bill Jr. and Thomas.

Soon after Pat's birth, the Ryans left Nevada. They moved to a small farm near Artesia, California. Their tiny house did not have electricity or running water.

Pat worked hard from a young age. Still, her family struggled to make a living.

On the farm, Bill began growing vegetables. He sold them to customers from the back of a truck. When she was old enough, Pat helped her father and brothers work in the fields. They harvested potatoes, tomatoes, peppers, cauliflower, peanuts, and other crops. Sometimes, Pat even drove a team of horses!

Determined Girl

Pat did not let her work keep her from getting an education. She walked one mile (2 km) to and from Pioneer Boulevard Grammar School. There, Pat was a successful student. She even skipped second grade.

Next, Pat attended Excelsior Union High School. Pat continued to do well in her studies there. She was a member of the drama club and acted in several school plays. Pat also joined the **debate** team. And, she served as student body secretary two years in a row.

Meanwhile, Pat's mother became ill with **cancer**. Pat cared for her and took over all the housework. This included cooking for her father, her brothers, and the seasonal farmworkers.

Sadly, Pat's mother died in January 1926. Afterward, Pat continued to manage the household while going to school. She made breakfast for her father and brothers. Then, she ran to catch her school bus. After school, Pat had more chores. She cleaned the house, washed clothes, and prepared dinner. Somehow, Pat still found time to study. In June 1929, she graduated at the top of her class.

Pat gained much early experience running a household. This prepared her for her later roles as a wife and a mother.

On Her Own

Soon after graduating from high school, Pat became an orphan. Her father had been sick with a lung disease. Though Pat nursed him for months, he died in May 1930.

At the time, the United States was suffering through the **Great Depression**. Pat had no money. Yet, she was determined to go to college. So, Pat took on whatever

As a young woman, Pat was eager to travel.

jobs she could find. First, she held a cleaning job. Then, she worked as a bank clerk. This helped her pay for classes at Fullerton Junior College. Pat attended Fullerton from 1931 to 1932.

In 1932, Pat accepted an unusual job. She drove an elderly couple from California to New York City, New York. The couple paid her with a return bus ticket to California. But when they

In New York, Pat held various jobs. These included an X-ray technician at a hospital and a secretary.

reached the East Coast, Pat decided to stay. She worked in New York for the next two years.

Pat moved back to California in 1934 and applied to college. She received a scholarship that paid for her schooling at the University of Southern California in Los Angeles. There, Pat studied **merchandising** and education.

In addition to her classes, Pat worked an average of 40 hours each week. She assisted a professor with a research project and grading student papers. Pat also worked as a sales clerk in a fancy department store. And, she played **extras** in several movies. Still, Pat graduated with **honors** in 1937.

Love and War

When Pat graduated from college, the nation was still in the **Great Depression**. Jobs were scarce, so Pat took the first one she was offered. She became a teacher at Whittier High School in Whittier, California. Pat taught typing and business classes there.

Pat also joined a community theater group called the Whittier Players. There, she met a lawyer named Richard Nixon. They both tried out for parts in a play called *The Dark Tower*.

Richard told Pat that someday she would marry

Richard proposed marriage to Pat in March 1940.

12

him. Yet Pat thought he was crazy. So, Richard courted her for more than two years. Finally on June 21, 1940, they married in Riverside, California. The couple then vacationed in Mexico.

Pat and Richard's wedding took place at the Mission Inn in Riverside, California.

After marrying Richard, Pat continued to teach. Then **World War II** interfered. On December 7, 1941, Japanese forces attacked the U.S. naval base at Pearl Harbor, Hawaii. The next day, the United States entered the war. Richard joined the U.S. Navy in 1942.

Pat accompanied her husband to various locations during his military training. Meanwhile, she worked for the American Red Cross and a bank. Then, Richard left to serve in the South Pacific. Pat moved to San Francisco, California. There, she worked for the U.S. government at the Office of Price Administration. World War II finally ended in 1945.

Wife and Mother

After Mr. Nixon returned from the war, the Nixons started a family. Their daughter Patricia was born on February 21, 1946. They called her Tricia.

Around the same time, Mr. Nixon entered politics. The **Republican** Party asked him to run for the U.S. House of Representatives. During the campaign, Mrs. Nixon researched the voting record of her husband's opponent. She also wrote information and handed it out to voters. She even spoke to voters at their homes. With her help, Mr. Nixon won the election!

In early 1947, the Nixon family moved to Washington, D.C. Mrs. Nixon would have preferred if her husband had chosen a different career. Yet, she could see it was the life he wanted. So, she stayed by his side to help. Mrs. Nixon even worked in her husband's office during his years in Congress. He spent four years in the House and two years in the U.S. Senate.

Meanwhile, the Nixons welcomed their second daughter. Julie was born on July 25, 1948. Mrs. Nixon wanted her children to have normal lives. So, she worked hard to keep her family's private life separate from politics.

Mrs. Nixon loved being a mother to Tricia (right) and Julie.

World Ambassador

In 1953, Mrs. Nixon's public role changed. That January, Mr. Nixon became vice president under President Dwight D. Eisenhower. Mrs. Nixon now made official appearances at luncheons and charity events. She also made time to visit hospitals, schools, orphanages, and senior citizen homes. She enjoyed connecting with Americans.

President Eisenhower recognized Mrs. Nixon's skill with people. So, he often had her accompany the vice president on trips abroad. Mrs. Nixon acted as a **goodwill** ambassador on these trips.

As a goodwill ambassador, Mrs. Nixon focused on helping others. During one trip to Japan, she gave a news conference for just female reporters. Mrs. Nixon knew this was a good opportunity for these women. Such an event had never occurred in Japan before.

Many of the countries the Nixons visited were Communist nations. At the time, these countries were rivals of the United States. In Venezuela, an angry mob threw rocks at Mr. and Mrs. Nixon's car. Yet, Mrs. Nixon stayed calm. Many newspaper reporters were impressed by her courage.

During her husband's time as vice president, Mrs. Nixon traveled to 53 countries. In each one, she visited schools and hospitals.

Back in the United States, Mrs. Nixon's reserved manner did not always earn her fans. In private, she was a charming and fun-loving woman. Yet, she was often uncomfortable in large groups and in public. This sometimes led Mrs. Nixon to appear stiff. Critics accused her of being cold and too formal. Some even called her "Plastic Pat."

Even so, many people felt Mrs. Nixon was the ideal traditional homemaker. **Conservative** women's groups approved of her simple style and support for her husband. In 1953, Mrs. Nixon was named Outstanding Homemaker of the Year. She earned the title Mother of the Year in 1955. And in 1957, she was named the Nation's Ideal Wife.

A campaign button from the 1968 presidential election

After eight years as vice president, Mr. Nixon ran several unsuccessful campaigns. Mrs. Nixon was disappointed at his losses. Yet, she was also relieved to have a quieter life. In 1963, the family moved to New York City so Mr. Nixon could practice law. Mrs. Nixon and her daughters were finally able to enjoy their privacy. However, it did not last.

In 1968, Mr. Nixon decided to run for president. At first, Mrs. Nixon was unhappy with this news. But soon, she was working tirelessly on her husband's campaign. She once said, "It takes heart to be in political life." That November, Mr. Nixon won the election!

By 1968, Mrs. Nixon had become an experienced campaigner. She drew many crowds, which helped her husband win the election.

Traveling First Lady

On January 20, 1969, Mrs. Nixon became First Lady. She was not sure how she would feel about this new role. Yet, she grew to like it. Mrs. Nixon especially enjoyed traveling the world again.

That July, Mrs. Nixon visited Vietnam. At the time, the **Vietnam War** was taking place. Mrs. Nixon became the first

In China, Mrs. Nixon met many people and saw many sights.

First Lady to enter a war zone since Eleanor Roosevelt. Mrs. Roosevelt had been First Lady during **World War II**.

In 1972, Mrs. Nixon made additional **goodwill** trips. She visited several African countries and met with their leaders. The Nixons also traveled together to China and the Soviet Union. In these Communist nations, the president attended political meetings. Meanwhile, the First Lady connected with the citizens there. She met with workers, students, farmers, and others.

Angel of Peru

In 1970, Mrs. Nixon journeyed to Peru. A tragic earthquake had struck there. Thousands of people were killed or left homeless. The First Lady delivered food, clothing, and medical supplies to the earthquake victims.

For her efforts, the Peruvian government gave Mrs. Nixon an award. It was called the Grand Cross of the Order of the Sun. This award is the highest decoration Peru can bestow. Mrs. Nixon was the first North American woman to receive this special honor.

At home, Mrs. Nixon spoke out for equal opportunities for men and women. Like many women at that time, she supported the **equal rights amendment**. She also supported appointing women to the U.S. **Supreme Court**. The First Lady was not afraid to stand up for changes in women's roles.

A White House for All

As First Lady, Mrs. Nixon devoted time to improving the White House. First Lady Jacqueline Kennedy had started a restoration project in 1961. Mrs. Nixon continued that work. She added hundreds of historic furnishings and works of art to the White House collection.

Mrs. Nixon wanted to make the White House available to more people, too. She added evening tours so daytime workers could visit the building. And, she had White House guides printed in multiple languages.

The First Lady also opened the White House to groups that had not been able to visit before. She had ramps installed for those with physical disabilities. She instructed tour guides to speak slowly. That way, **hearing-impaired** people could read their lips. She also allowed blind visitors to touch many valuable White House objects.

Mrs. Nixon knew the importance of connecting with Americans. So, she took time to personally greet White House visitors. She shook their hands and signed **autographs**. The First Lady also received thousands of letters each week. She took several hours each day to read as many as she could.

Mrs. Nixon worked hard to furnish the White House. She collected about 600 paintings and pieces of historic furniture for the mansion.

An Early Good-bye

In 1972, Mrs. Nixon supported her husband's successful campaign for a second term. Not long after, the Watergate **scandal** captured the nation's attention. Earlier that year, some **Republicans** had hired burglars to break into the Watergate building in Washington, D.C. They had wanted information to help the president's reelection campaign. Afterward, they had tried to cover up the break-in.

President Nixon knew about the cover-up, but he tried to deny his involvement. Mrs. Nixon had always given advice to her husband. Yet, the president kept his family in the dark about Watergate. Mrs. Nixon learned about the scandal from the newspapers.

The First Lady believed her husband was innocent. But after months of investigations, President Nixon was unable to clear his name. So in July 1974, Mrs. Nixon began preparing to leave the White House.

On August 9, President Nixon resigned. In his farewell speech to his staff, the president thanked many people. But he failed to mention his wife. Mrs. Nixon was hurt, but she continued to support her husband. She faced the Watergate scandal with much grace.

After the Nixons left the White House, Vice President
Gerald Ford (left) became U.S. president.

Final Years

The challenges of political life had pressured Mr. and Mrs. Nixon's marriage. The Nixons quietly retired to San Clemente, California. Once there, Mrs. Nixon withdrew from public life.

In 1976, Mrs. Nixon suffered a **stroke**. The stroke partially **paralyzed** her left arm and leg. It also paralyzed the left side of her face. Mrs. Nixon worked hard to recover. Slowly, she regained most of her movement.

The Nixons settled on the East Coast in 1981. Mrs. Nixon spent her time reading, gardening, and visiting her family. Mr. Nixon attempted to mend his political career.

In 1983, Mrs. Nixon suffered another stroke. She recovered, but then her health began to worsen. She battled **emphysema** and then lung **cancer**. Mrs. Nixon died on June 22, 1993, at her home in Park Ridge, New Jersey. She was buried at the Richard Nixon Library & Birthplace in Yorba Linda, California.

Mr. and Mrs. Nixon continued to count on each other for support through the years.

Patricia Nixon was a dedicated wife, mother, and First Lady. She worked hard throughout her life and always tried to do the right thing. Today, Mrs. Nixon may be most remembered for leaving the White House after the Watergate **scandal**. However, her many **goodwill** missions at home and abroad should never be forgotten.

Timeline

1912	On March 16, Thelma Catherine "Pat" Ryan was born.
1929	Pat graduated from Excelsior Union High School at the top of her class.
1931–1932	Pat attended Fullerton Junior College.
1937	Pat graduated with honors from the University of Southern California.
1940	Pat married Richard Nixon on June 21.
1946	On February 21, the Nixons' daughter Patricia, or Tricia, was born.
1948	On July 25, the Nixons' daughter Julie was born.
1953–1961	While Mr. Nixon served as Dwight D. Eisenhower's vice president, Mrs. Nixon acted as a goodwill ambassador.
1969–1974	Mrs. Nixon acted as First Lady, while her husband served as U.S. president.
1969	In July, Mrs. Nixon visited a war zone in Vietnam.
1972	Mrs. Nixon traveled to Africa; the Nixons traveled to China and the Soviet Union; President Nixon won reelection; the Watergate scandal captured the nation's attention.
1974	On August 9, President Nixon resigned from office.
1993	Mrs. Nixon died on June 22.

Did You Know?

Patricia Nixon sold part of her father's farm to help pay for her husband's first campaign. She had also been saving money to buy a home. Instead, she gave it to the campaign effort.

Mrs. Nixon was often rated in Gallup opinion polls. Every year from 1968 to 1971, she was named one of the nation's most admired women.

Until First Lady Hillary Clinton, Mrs. Nixon was the most traveled First Lady. She visited more than 80 countries between 1969 and 1974.

Mrs. Nixon was the first First Lady to appear in public wearing pants.

Mrs. Nixon was the first Republican First Lady to address the Republican National Convention. She gave her speech in 1972, when her husband was renominated for president.

Mrs. Nixon's childhood home near Artesia is now the site of Pat Nixon Park. On March 1, 1997, a statue of Mrs. Nixon was dedicated there. It is one of the first life-size statues of a First Lady.

Glossary

autograph - a person's handwritten name.

cancer - any of a group of often deadly diseases marked by an abnormal growth of cells that destroys healthy tissues and organs.

conservative - relating to someone who has traditional beliefs and often dislikes change.

debate - a contest in which two sides argue for or against something.

emphysema (ehm-fuh-ZEE-muh) - a condition marked by enlarged air spaces in the lungs and shortness of breath. It often leads to a weakened heart.

equal rights amendment - a proposed change to the U.S. Constitution that would guarantee equal rights to males and females.

extra - a person hired to act in a group scene in a movie.

goodwill - kindly interest, friendliness, support, or concern.

Great Depression - the period from 1929 to 1942 of worldwide economic trouble. There was little buying or selling, and many people could not find work.

hearing-impaired - having reduced hearing ability.

honors - special attention given to a graduating student for high academic achievement.

merchandising - the practice of improving sales of goods or services through effective advertising and attractive presentation.

paralyze - to cause a loss of motion or feeling in a part of the body.

Republican - a member of the Republican political party. Republicans are conservative and believe in small government.

scandal - an action that shocks people and disgraces those connected with it.

stroke - a sudden loss of consciousness, sensation, and voluntary motion. This attack of paralysis is caused by a rupture to a blood vessel of the brain, often caused by a blood clot.

Supreme Court - the highest, most powerful court in the United States.

Vietnam War - from 1957 to 1975. A long, failed attempt by the United States to stop North Vietnam from taking over South Vietnam.

World War II - from 1939 to 1945, fought in Europe, Asia, and Africa. Great Britain, France, the United States, the Soviet Union, and their allies were on one side. Germany, Italy, Japan, and their allies were on the other side.

Web Sites

To learn more about Patricia Nixon, visit ABDO Publishing Company on the World Wide Web at **www.abdopublishing.com**. Web sites about Patricia Nixon are featured on our Book Links page. These links are routinely monitored and updated to provide the most current information available.

Index